Hallel

Hallelujah Joe

One Man's Journey from Crime to Christ

JOE SCHARWÄCHTER

Translated by
Morag McFeat

Preface by
Colonel Bramwell Booth

MarshallPickering
An Imprint of HarperCollins*Publishers*

Marshall Pickering
An Imprint of HarperCollins*Religious*
Part of HarperCollins*Publishers*
77–85 Fulham Palace Road,
Hammersmith
London W6 8JB

Originally published in Germany
Copyright © 1989 Brendow Verlag, D-4130 Moers-1 Germany
First published in English in
Great Britain by Marshall Pickering 1991

Copyright © The General of the Salvation Army 1990
English translation copyright ©
HarperCollins*Publishers* 1991

The Author asserts the moral right to
be identified as the author of this work

A catalogue record for this book is
available from the British Library

ISBN 0 551 02424 0

Typeset by Medcalf Type Ltd, Bicester, Oxon

Printed and bound in Great Britain by
HarperCollins Manufacturing Glasgow

This book is sold subject to the condition that it shall not, by way of trade of otherwise, be lent, re-sold, hired out or otherwise circulated without the publisher's prior consent in any form of binding or cover other than that in which it is published and without a similar condition including this condition being imposed on the subsequent purchaser.

Contents

PREFACE vii

INTRODUCTION 1

One
RUNAWAY AGED THREE 5

Two
SCHOOLDAYS 9

Three
FUGITIVE 11

Four
CONFIRMATION CLASSES 15

Five
LEARNING THE TRICKS OF THE TRADE 20

Six
MY FIRST CONVICTED ROBBERY AND FIRST REAL PRISON STINT 24

Seven
ESCAPE TO AFRICA 28

Eight
MY INTRODUCTION TO PROSTITUTION 31

Nine
MY MOTHER DIES 35

Ten
UNLUCKY IN LOVE 39

Eleven
A PIMP IN FRANKFURT 43

Twelve
DOING TIME 51

Thirteen
SHALL I BE YOUR PROSTITUTE? 56

Fourteen
DEFLATED AND DESPONDENT 59

Fifteen
MY DREAM WOMAN 62

Sixteen
MY CONVERSION 64

Seventeen
THE FINAL CONSEQUENCE 66

Eighteen
DOES SHE LOVE ME? 69

Nineteen
TURNED DOWN AND TAKEN ON 72

Twenty
BREAKING WITH THE PAST 74

Twenty-one
A NEW START IN FREEDOM 77

Twenty-two
JOIN THE SALVATION ARMY? NOT A CHANCE! 80

Twenty-three
HALLELUJAH 87

Twenty-four
ENROLLED 91

Twenty-five
THE SAGA OF MY DRIVING LICENCE 94

Twenty-six
SERVING THE LORD AND MORE 98

EPILOGUE 105

Preface

Captain Scharwächter's conversion was one of many unexpected developments in the life of a petty criminal, but it has totally transformed the personality and comportment of a man destined apparently to life-imprisonment.

It was not the German police which finally arrested his headlong rush into hell but the Spirit of God who turned him into an unusual but effective evangelist and made him 'a prisoner of the Lord', as St Paul once testified. Evangelical campaigns which have brought tens of thousands face to face with the challenge which Christ brings to our lives have resulted in hundreds of men and women experiencing, in their turn, the transformation of conversion.

Captain Jo Scharwächter's beginnings were hard, and his writing reflects the brutality of his early years but allows us to learn of the immense patience and compassion of God in bringing him into a new and living way.

Jo Scharwächter's battle was the hardest challenge he had to face, but one which he won triumphantly. May his life's story inspire many to know also the life-transforming experience of conversion.

BRAMWELL BOOTH
Colonel
Territorial Commander – Germany

INTRODUCTION

Surname Scharwächter. First name Joachim Nickname: Joe. Born on 23 March 1944 in Helmond (The Netherlands). Married with three children. Criminal prosecutions for pimping, armed robbery, theft, grievous bodily harm, driving without a current licence. Total term of imprisonment nine-and-a-half years. Present career Salvation Army Officer.

These are my personal details according to official records but there is a lot more colour and excitement to my life, and a lot of contradictions in my character that have led me to experience a whole range of human opposites. I have known evil and violence and put myself in dangerous situations, and yet I am weak and sentimental and a lover of beauty. I have laughed as well as cried, although at one point in life I swore to bury my emotions for ever and never shed another tear ever again. From a very early age I started running away from home over and over again. Inside there was a deep-rooted urge to escape as far away as possible. But I always got caught and locked up in homes, reform schools or borstals. I have always had an uneasy love-hate relationship with women, finding it easy to take them to bed,

Hallelujah Joe

and make them prostitute themselves to support me, I have beaten girlfriends. And yet now I am truly in love with just one woman, my wife. I have sat confined within grey prison walls and yet have also enjoyed complete freedom bathed in the bright sunshine of the Mediterranean. I have been an alcoholic and now I do not touch a drop. In the past I have used my fists to defend myself, and nowadays I preach the love of God. I have acted tough and often fled God's presence but I have crawled back on my knees before him on the cross, and shouted out to him to forgive my sins for I had truly strayed from the path of righteousness. And I have rejoiced in the joy of his forgiveness, crying out Hallelujah.

I am well known for my habit of crying out Hallelujah. It is for this reason that I am nicknamed 'Hallelujah Joe'. Before then I was referred to as Dutch Joe in the criminal circle within which I moved, but I left that life behind me and donned the Salvation Army uniform, travelling the length and breadth of the country to preach. I meet and speak to all walks of life from down and outs, prostitutes and crooks to housewives, managing directors and civil servants. I am willing to tell everyone who wants to know or even those who do not want to listen about the person who so radically altered my life, Jesus Christ. Because I know from personal experience that deep down in everyone there is a dark side that can be lit up by his light.

Introduction

It is because now the joy of Christ that I want everyone to share my story, or more explicitly the story of my two lives before and after my conversion. The story of a pimp who found a fairy tale but a true account of how a harsh, dark existence tinged with violence became enriched through God's presence and how I found lasting happiness.

Chapter One

RUNAWAY AGED THREE

I was born on 23 March 1944 along with my twin brother Kurt one year before the end of the Second World War in the town of Helmond in Holland. Right from the cradle I was called 'Dutch Joe'. My parents, Kurt and Anita Scharwächter, had moved to Holland in 1937. They owned a small hosiery. In 1938 their first-born child Heide was born and on the outbreak of war my father joined the army. I never knew him for he fell in action in Russia six weeks after our birth. My mother later told me that on hearing of his death she wanted to kill herself. She had no idea how she was going to cope bringing up three young children on her own, especially in Holland where she had no relatives to lend a helping hand. As the allies advanced freeing occupied Holland we were deported back to Germany, to Wuppertal where my mother had been born.

There the four of us lived cramped together in a small, dank two-bedroomed flat. From time to time we were joined by a variety of fifth members and we were encouraged by my mother to call these strangers 'uncle'. In those days this kind of occurrence was not uncommon. Many husbands had perished in the war leaving their wives alone and

Hallelujah Joe

lonely, with or without children to tend. I often heard from friends in our street when they had a new 'uncle' on the go. My mother worked herself to the point of exhaustion, like so many other women in the postwar years, just for the sake of her children. The state provided her with single-parent benefit and child allowance but both these could not make ends meet. So she was forced to find work wherever she could, in factories, in the post office or any cleaning jobs. So long as it paid she took it, and as children we were often left on our own to fend for ourselves. If she was not working she was sick, often plagued by thrombosis.

It soon became clear to my sister Heide and myself that we had drawn the short straw for my mother made no attempt to hide the fact that Kurt, the baby of the family, was her favourite. She spoilt him rotten, showering him with all sorts of goodies whilst we had to content ourselves with his discarded toys. Indeed we were lucky if we got anything at all. From birth he had always been the weaker twin, often sickly and therefore given the extra care and attention that both my sister and I craved. We were constantly fobbed off whilst she devoted herself to his every whim. There was no doubting that Kurt had never been in the best of health. He was also a very accident-prone child, managing once to break his ankle just by falling down. Everything that could possibly go wrong with a child happened to him.

Despite his inadequacies or maybe even because

of them, he remained the firm favourite with my mother. One Christmas he was presented with a brand new bicycle whereas I was handed a beat-up scooter and a pair of football boots four sizes too big. Heide and I learned not to grumble. We knew after a while if we put up any protest about being unfairly treated it would just be levelled against us that Kurt was in a worse state of health and had a much tougher time at school than either of us. To her we were like our poor dead father, whereas Kurt took after her more. Somehow she never fully learned to accept that our father had not returned from the war and we were living reminders of this loss. Her favouritism for Kurt never waned and died with her two weeks before our 18th birthday.

To this day my sister and I still feel the pain her rejection of us and her neglect which forced us to argue and quarrel. At eighteen, Heide could not bear any more and left home to settle in East Germany. Today she lives in Spain. I too harboured strong feelings of hatred and resentment towards my mother from a very early age. There is no doubt that my getting into trouble and my constant need to run away can be linked directly to my unhappy home life and problematic relationship with my mother.

I was only three years of age the first time I headed out of the flat on my own and set off down the street towards the cable railway. I climbed the steps up to the local station and boarded the next tram

Hallelujah Joe

eventually getting off at the end stop. There I grabbed a complete stranger by the hand and told him, 'Uncle, I need a pee-pee.' The police took me home but my mother never let me forget this, casting it up it every time I was brought home from other run-away attempts in later childhood.

Chapter Two

SCHOOLDAYS

Because Kurt was such a weakling we could not go to school until we were seven, a year later than normal. Secretly I always held this against him for I was desperately keen to go to school but was kept back because of him. Our first day at school was nevertheless quite an event, for five sets of twins enrolled on the same day. Our picture appeared in the newspaper holding our gigantic conical bags of sweeties, which every German schoolchild is given on their first day at school. For the first time in my life I found myself at the centre of attention and I loved it.

For the first four years at school I was an average pupil of changeable abilities dependent on my attitude. A hindering factor was my poor relationship with my teacher. We did not get on with each other in the slightest. She was biased against me because she had already taught my sister Heide, who despite being bright was also a difficult child. My teacher never let me forget this and there was nothing I could do to alter her opinion. When I got too fed up with the situation, I simply skipped school. Sometimes I stayed away for up to three weeks. At home I made up some story to cover myself. Nowadays such behaviour is detected early and dealt with but at the beginning of the fifties there were no questions asked.

It was proved during my third year at school that I was well capable of achieving better results. My uncle on my mother's side decided to take me under his wing. He was headmaster of a village school, had no children of his own and wanted to help out my mother. So for three years he agreed to keep me for half the year and at his school I passed all my exams with flying colours because I was motivated. But in the other six months, back in Wuppertal, my marks plummeted again because I hated my teacher so much.

By primary four things had deteriorated to the point that I kicked my teacher hard on the shins one day and that was the end. I could not face going back to her class and played truant for over a fortnight. Then my report card was issued warning, of course, that I was likely to be kept back a year due to my prolonged absences. My mother had no alternative but to move me to another school.

I was placed in a convent school. It was like a day school. We had lessons in the morning, then after lunch we did our homework until it was time to go home in the evening. Right from the start things improved. I was given nearly top marks for my first essay. I had great respect for my teacher, whom we all nicknamed 'Beanpole'. I thought she was fantastic and I will never forget how much I liked her. However, even although my attitude towards school had changed this did not prevent me from continuing to run away from home.

Chapter Three

FUGITIVE

In the autumn of 1956 when I was twelve years old I went on my first major trip to Holland. In the past I had spent six weeks' summer holidays there at my Aunt Jo's. She had nine children and owned a guesthouse. Life there was great. I could eat as much as I wanted, play football and generally let off steam. The family was well respected in the town and Aunt Jo treated me exactly like one of her own children. Back in Wuppertal whenever things began to get on top of me I would often reminisce on the good times at my aunt's.

A year later, life in Wuppertal with all its pressures became too much to bear and I convinced myself that there would be no problem in going to live with my aunt Jo permanently. I would be well behaved and in a family of ten another child is neither here nor there, or so I thought. I stole a bicycle from a younger boy and pedalled off. It was an overcast, foggy day with outbreaks of rain. I felt heavy at heart and I stopped to ponder for a while for I realized I was making a big decision and the course I was taking was probably irreversible.

Eventually I pulled myself together and cycled on, always looking forward, never back. I kept pedalling

Hallelujah Joe

in more or less the right direction for I managed to piece together the route from recalling the names of stations we had passed through on previous train journeys. I followed traffic signs for Düsseldorf, Mönchen-Gladbach, Kaldenkirchen and then the border.

At first it was hard work up and down dale for it is a mountainous region but after Düsseldorf the going got a lot easier. I stole a few things to eat en route, like some apples from a market stall. The total journey from Wuppertal to the border was over 100km but by the afternoon I had already reached Kaldenkirchen, the nearest town to the border.

I was so green that I thought I could simply ride across the border so I went right up to the barrier on my stolen bicycle. I was automatically questioned by a border guard, or it might even have been a customs official. I told him I was on my way to visit my aunt in Helmond but he doubted that my parents would allow me to travel there on my own. I cheekily assured him that I had their consent but I was stumped when he asked me for proof and my identity card.

My mother had of course applied for the necessary child passes the last time without my knowledge and she would have shown these papers at the border checkpoint but in my excitement I had not noticed this exchange. Now by going it alone I had fallen head first into the trap. Now the guard knew for sure that I had run away.

The full brunt of the law bore down on me. I was

Fugitive

detained and cross-questioned. All my attempts to wriggle out through lying were to no avail. The truth was dragged out of me and the bicycle was confiscated. The whole episode in the guardroom lasted for hours whilst a whole series of guards came to eye me up and pose awkward questions. Telephone calls were made and advice given to me but all the time anger was steadily welling up inside me, directed more at my own stupidity than at my official treatment. I swore blind that I would never be caught out like this again.

It was late in the evening when I was taken to a shelter for young offenders in Krefeld. It was a gloomy building and this was to be my first taste of what it feels like to be imprisoned. I was put into a dormitory on the first floor with bunk beds and stale air. I decided straight away that I could not stomach such a place, still bitter and disappointed that my journey an plans for a better future had come to such an abrupt end. At night when all was quiet I climbed out the window, and hanging from the guttering jumped down to the ground and scarpered. No-one had seen me leave.

I travelled only by night. During the day I hid from the police, mainly taking cover in woods, sleeping out under bushes. It was icily cold and damp. On top of this I had to look to where my next meal was coming from for I had to eat. What saved me from starvation was the early morning bread and milk deliveries which were left out on the doorsteps. This service no longer exists in Germany but luckily for me was still active then in the fifties for a person can survive quite adequately on this staple diet.

I eventually arrived back in Wuppertal about a week later but I did not dare go home for I knew that the police would be there lying in wait for me. So I spent the next six weeks on the streets, sleeping rough in condemned houses or on building sites and stealing anything I could lay my hands on. I finally got caught red-handed, driven to carelessness out of sheer hunger. I had broken into a fruit shop one night without even noticing that it was right next door to the local police station. They must have been attracted by the noise I was making, so once again I was caught by the scruff of the neck and marched off for questioning. It did not take them long to work out who I was and I was thankfully taken back home at last. There not only my mother was waiting for me but also a youth welfare officer.

Chapter Four

CONFIRMATION CLASSES

I was assigned to a child welfare officer because I now had a police record of being a runaway and petty thief. My mother quite understandably washed her hands of me and I was made to attend a so-called boarding school. In fact this was just a glorified description for what was in effect a reform school.

I was placed in a Protestant children's home in Bad Godesberg, directed by a church minister. Everyone was divided into groups and we all slept in enormous dormitories but on the whole it was not so bad. Coping with homesickness was the worst. I just longed to be in a home environment and therefore constantly tried to escape and make my way back to Wuppertal. Because I was now adept at being a runaway I succeeded in getting home a couple of times but I was never allowed to stay for any length of time.

For me perhaps the most painful part of life in the home was watching the other children opening letters or even parcels from their parents, especially on their birthdays. I never received any mail, not a single line, not even a bar of chocolate as a present, nothing. My mother made absolutely no attempt to keep in touch with me. She cut me off completely.

Hallelujah Joe

I did not want the other children to find out that I was the odd one out, and that unlike them I could not share out things from parcel, so I stole things to give away instead. For example, on a school outing to Rothenburg I went shoplifting. I ought to have learnt by then that crime never pays and eventually I would get caught, and of course I did get caught. I was summoned to the headmaster's office to be duly punished. Bent double I was given ten or maybe even fifteen of the best from a long leather strap. It really hurt and I was furious but I did not blame the headmaster for doling out the correct punishment to fit the crime. I was mad at myself that I had allowed myself to be detected.

A couple of years later my mother telephoned me out of the blue for the first time ever. She said my brother Kurt had just been confirmed and she wanted me to take my vows too. On this we did not see eye to eye for it was not important to me and why should I do anything just to please her? I immediately said no.

I had not had a particularly religious upbringing and indeed had never shown much interest in such matters. This is not to say that we did not attend church from time to time for we went at Christmas, Easter and maybe a couple of other occasions throughout the year. The day school I had gone to in Wuppertal for a short time had religious lessons as part of the curriculum so we also went to children's church services now and again. During this period I was particularly influenced by a black

Confirmation Classes

American singer, Kenneth Spencer. His son attended our school and sometimes, for instance at Christmas, his father would sing beautiful songs, spirituals or German Christmas carols. The fact alone that he was a coloured person was a big enough sensation for me at the time but the fact that he also handed out chocolate bars to everyone really made me like him even more. Later I learned he had died in an air crash over New Orleans. But it was Spencer who basically aroused a positive interest in Christianity. My brother went along to a Christian youth group so I went along with him, even to a few missionary meetings but to be honest I can hardly remember anything about them.

In our catechism classes I devised a plan to test whether the minister actually practised what he preached about the love of God and love thy neighbour. In the next lesson I let off a stink bomb under his desk and how did he react? He slapped me across the face on both cheeks and banished me from attending his class.

And now my mother wanted me to be confirmed because it was the done thing and because Kurt was confirmed. My instant refusal was countered by the offer of a bribe of a suit of my own and also a watch. These material goods were not things that any fourteen-year old would wish to turn down so I relented and gave in to her wish.

In place of the usual two years of lessons I sat a crash course on religion. I had to learn the hymn 'Holy God, we praise thy name', and a reading from the Letter of Paul to the Philippians, Philippians verses 5-11: 'Let your bearing towards one another arise out of your life in Christ Jesus. For the divine nature was his from the first, yet he did not think to snatch at equality with God, but made himself nothing, assuming the nature of a slave. Bearing the human likeness, revealed in human shape, he humbled himself, and in obedience accepted even death – death on a cross. Therefore God raised him to the heights and bestowed on him the name above all names, that at the name of Jesus every knee should bow – in heaven, on earth, and in the depths – and every tongue confess, "Jesus Christ is Lord", to the glory of God the Father.'

Quite a mouthful for a young boy to memorize and recite. I somehow never forgot this passage even although its true meaning did not hit me until many years later. At the time it was purely an exercise to help me win the material prize of a suit and watch. On the day of my confirmation I was asked to the manse where the minister and a group of presbyters had assembled to hear my renditions and having passed I was allowed to be put forward for confirmation.

It was no bother to me at all. I could not imagine how my brother had taken two years of confirmation classes to do what I had done in a matter of minutes. After the church ceremony there was a big celebration at home in my honour. One of the bedrooms was emptied of its furniture to make room for the hordes of relatives that descended on the flat,

Confirmation Classes

many of whom I had never seen before. I felt wretched, a stranger in my own family. Not even my sister Heide was there because she had now been in East Germany for over two years. My brother on the other hand was very much at home, compounding my feelings of hurt at being excluded from the family unit. He lived here in person but I only lived here in spirit.

Chapter Five

LEARNING THE TRICKS OF THE TRADE

After my confirmation I went through the usual pattern of questioning as to what I wanted to do in life. I had not fixed on any real career plans, the only thing I knew was that I could not go back to school because I had failed the entrance examination to go on to further education. The only option open to me now was to take up an apprenticeship, so my mother found me a placement with a organ maker.

I enjoyed this work but despite my interest I only lasted at it for five months. Not that I had any problems getting on with my instructor. I applied myself and wanted to learn. But fate dealt me a bitter blow. My health deteriorated. I started to suffer from chronic diarrhoea and on a few occasions had to get signed off by the doctor. After two days at home I would recover completely but one day back at work and the symptoms returned. My illness was a medical mystery until the doctor struck on the idea that it was due to a chemical reaction. My main task as the apprentice was to clean the keys with paraffin oil and evidently I was allergic to the smell. So it made no sense to carry on in this trade. I had to leave.

Learning the Tricks of the Trade

I was given another apprenticeship as a locksmith but I did not take to it the same. Moreover I was having problems at home. I earned thirty-five marks a month. This was a lot of money in those days, but I had to hand over all but 8 marks to my mother and out of it I was compelled to buy my mother flowers for a further 2 marks, otherwise she would not have allowed me to retain a penny of my own. It was not a fair situation for my brother did not have to give up any of his wages or pay anything towards lodgings. It is not surprising that I felt victimized and arguments arose.

We could not resolve our differences so after a while my mother informed me that she had been in touch with the social services and she had arranged with a youth welfare officer for me to go into a neighbouring reform school if I would prefer to go. Part of the deal was that I could come home at weekends and I would be trained up in the apprenticeship of my choice within the school facilities.

I decided to give it a go and unwittingly landed up in Halveshof in a school for the maladjusted. This proved to be a great shock to me and acted as a catalyst in my life. Instead of learning a respectable, professional trade, the foundations were cemented there for a life of crime.

The very first impressions were lasting. There was no friendly reception on arrival but we were all filed into an assembly point. There were no bedrooms or dormitories as such, only tiny cells with bars on

Hallelujah Joe

the windows. We were stripped of our personal clothing which had to be handed in and replaced by standard grey overalls and heavy duty black shoes and we were also given floor cloths, to mop up. We were treated very badly. Getting smacked across the face was a regular occurrence, as was being beaten about the ribcage, punched in the stomach or thumped on the nose. All punishments for the least offence were meted out by our so-called teachers. Those who were foolish enough not to bow to authority or those who could not defend themselves had to suffer the further indignity of homosexual abuse. Absolutely shocking things that would make your mind boggle went on within these walls.

Of course great emphasis was placed on religious education for it was a Christian institution. Every Sunday we were trooped off to church. There was no escaping this because if you did not attend you were not allowed out at all. This nurtured a strong feeling of resentment and I began to hate all Christians and Christianity itself. I can still see myself sitting on a pew, dressed in my scruffy uniform and looking up at the minister as he spoke of love and of Jesus and I knew shortly afterwards he would be openly beating us. I transferred his hypocritical behaviour on to the values of Christianity and I wanted nothing to do with him or it. If I could have hit back in any way I would have done so.

At Halveshof they had an odd way of operating. You first had to prove your worth at making carpets before you were considered for any other training.

Learning the Tricks of the Trade

Tying knots in rough hemp shredded your hands until they bled. You were promised a move to the carpentry department if you did well and achieved a certain target. For days I offered little resistance and accepted my fate. At night I cried myself to sleep and was ridiculed by the other boys. They beat me up and when I fought back I was given another thrashing. After a while I sharpened up and got friendly with some of the older boys for protection. From them I learned all the tricks of the trade, from how to break into a car and start it up to full-fledged burglary. I undertook a whole foundation course in criminality, taught by experts. The theory completed, myself and two other boys about my age decided to put the methods into practice. The first step was to take the door off its hinges and head off. What we had not remembered in this instance was that we were all still wearing our conspicuous grey uniforms.

Chapter Six

MY FIRST CONVICTED ROBBERY AND FIRST REAL PRISON STINT

It was midnight when we made our escape. Outside it was pitch black. We crept through the woods, heading first towards the Müngsten bridge in Solingen and then on to Wuppertal. As morning dawned we were already feeling pretty hungry. We saw a woman approaching carrying two heavy shopping bags. I went up to her and asked if she had anything there for us to eat but she said she had nothing. By this time my mates had edged in on her. I asked again whether she at least had some money she could give us. She looked at us intimidated and with trembling hands dug into her handbag. Eventually she managed to pull out her purse and handed it to me. I shook out the contents and pocketed the total of two marks and ninety-five pfennigs, mumbling my thanks at now being able to buy something to eat. Leaving her rooted to the spot we sloped off thinking no more about it for we genuinely thought the woman had given us the money of her own accord.

Quarter of an hour later the police drew up beside us in a patrol car and asked us if we had stopped

My First Robbery and First Real Prison Stint

a woman and asked her for money. We admitted to this immediately and were taken down the local station and interrogated individually. We were asked to recount the exact sequence of events. Did we threaten the woman? Did we rip the purse out of her hand. And so on and so forth for the whole length of the day. That evening we were locked up in a detention centre in Wuppertal.

It was a terrible experience. I still have nightmares whenever I think about it. We were only fifteen and still in our short trousers. These were replaced by smelly overalls and then we were split up into different cell blocks so that we could not collaborate. Being marginally the oldest of the three I was put in the adult section, a huge grey building with long corridors and a multitude of doors that had to be unlocked and locked behind us as we went. The cell itself was little more than a dark shell with a window placed so high up that the light never fully penetrated and you could only catch a glimpse of sky through the thick iron bars. It was kitted out with a steel bed, little cupboard and wash basin. There was no toilet but for the customary bucket in the corner. Here you were locked up for twenty-three hours a day with the remaining hour spent in the exercise yard. Later on we were given work to do, making press-studs from early morning till night time. The work never varied and the younger boys were given set quotas to achieve and paid ten to twenty pfennigs an hour (5p maximum) so by the end of the month we had earned a few marks.

Hallelujah Joe

Not for the first time in my life I felt totally alone and isolated. Again I did not receive a single letter from my mother, not a postcard, not a parcel, the usual blank. It was as if I had ceased to exist for my family even though I was still only fifteen and in trouble. I found out in the exercise yard that my two accomplices had been sent parcels from their homes which made me feel even more deprived and cut-off. I even wrote home to my mother pleading with her to send me something or some word but she did not reply. Then with Christmas coming I perked up like everybody else looking forward to the celebrations, thinking she was bound to think about me then. But not so much as a Christmas card arrived.

I can still picture myself standing under the window in my cell knowing that only a few hundred yards away as the crow flies my mother and brother would be standing by the Christmas tree at home singing 'Silent Night' and unpacking their presents. The image tore me apart. I felt totally abandoned. The tears welled up inside but I struggled with all my might to hold them back. It was at that point that I swore to myself that I would never cry again. No one could hurt me as much as this again and no one should ever find out just how deeply I had been wounded. I could not think about my brother without a hatred brought on by intense jealousy. How did he manage to get on so well with my mother when all I could do was fight with her? I began even to hate my mother because she behaved

My First Robbery and First Real Prison Stint

as though she had only one son. She did not love me and it was me that needed her love most. At that moment of realization I grew up. Outwardly I still resembled the child I was but inwardly my heart had hardened, all compassion froze and the seeds of bitterness that were to gnaw at me for years to come were sown.

The next morning in the prison Christmas church service when the congregation sang 'Open up the door, the gateway to heaven is wide' I fled the church and begged to be locked back in my cell for I despised the thought of church people crying because they felt lonely.

I could not make any sense of the world any more. I could not understand even why I was in prison in the first place, far less punished in this way. I had only asked the woman for something to eat. Where was her Christian goodness?

Chapter Seven
ESCAPE TO AFRICA

In February 1960 a few weeks before my sixteenth birthday our trial hearing was called. I stood in the dock along with my two mates and looking around I was astonished to see my mother sitting on a spectators' bench. The charge was read out 'Robbery with resort to violence'. The prosecuting attorney showed no mercy. From the outset he made continuous reference to our past offenses and intimated that we were destined to lead a life of crime. He recommended draconian sentences which were duly meted out to us. One of the boys was an orphan and consequently was given two to four years, dependent on behaviour, in a borstal. The other was given a similar sentence of three years. For being the main culprit I escaped with the lightest sentence of 18 months detention less our remand time in custody, the balance suspended to a three year probationary period. So I could leave the courtroom there and then and go straight home.

But I was not exactly free because I was boxed in by public opinion. Everyone I came in contact with knew I had been inside and now had a criminal record. No one trusted me any more. Whenever anything went wrong in the slightest the immediate

Escape to Africa

blame fell on me. If ever I did anything to displease my mother in any way, such as coming home later than expected, she threatened me with the prospect of going back to prison by having a word with my probation officer about my general behaviour. She took advantage of the situation to exercise her power over me. In a way it was worse than prison. For a while I let it wash over me, ignoring all her reproaches until it all got on top of me. I could not care less any more what she said to me or what she thought of me. I wanted out. I tried to find work but everywhere I turned the barriers were up. No one wanted to give me a break. I felt stifled and needed to get out of this oppressive atmosphere so every weekend I used to take to the roads, hitchhiking. I went all over Germany and as far as Austria and back. This was the only pleasure I had in life. I was caught in the lure of faraway places.

One morning I informed my mother that I was off to visit my uncle near Kassel as I needed a change of scenery. I lied to her when I said I had been given a few days holiday. She did not know that I had been given my notice weeks ago and in the meantime I had been shoplifting and hawking the proceeds to pay the percentage of my previous wage she demanded and have a little bit over for myself.

This time I set off with the objective of getting as far away as possible and not coming back. I now had a passport which my mother had agreed to let me keep. Within no time at all I had hitched a lift all the way to Saragossa in Spain. As the miles

Hallelujah Joe

slipped away and we got further and further from Wuppertal the more relieved I felt. At last I could leave everything behind me. No one knew I was on probation so there was no one to quiz me on my misdeeds and no one had any reason to mistrust me. I got to know a lot of people, adventurers like myself. Sometimes I was invited back to their homes for dinner and treated like an equal. It was a completely new experience for me.

From Saragossa I headed toward Malaga, taking any available means of transport from motorbikes to articulated lorries. On reaching the docks I asked around for news of a ship bound for Africa and amazingly found it relatively easy to work my passage. I was taken on almost immediately as a deck hand, scrubbing them down all day and doing all the necessary dirty work until we docked in Morocco. I had been away five weeks before I wrote my first postcard home from Africa. My sister was on a visit to Wuppertal at the time this postcard arrived and she later informed me that my mother had aged by years in that period for she had no idea whether I was alive or dead.

From Morocco I made it down to Algeria, still managing to find lifts. My plan was to join the Foreign Legion. I was even given an interview because I looked eighteen or nineteen but I blew my chance when I naively told them my real age. I still had a lot to learn. I could not stay there so I more or less backtracked along the same path I had taken on the way down through Spain again and went up into France.

Chapter Eight

MY INTRODUCTION TO PROSTITUTION

I was standing by the side of a country road outside Toulouse trying to hitch my next lift when a motorbike screeched to a halt. The biker dressed all in black invited me to hop on. He was a Catholic priest. During the journey, however, he kept slipping his hand backwards and stroking my ankle. There was not much I could do to fight him off especially on such a winding bumpy road. He took me to a church administrative building where there were also guest rooms and said he wold put me up there for the night. He even introduced me to a bishop. Then the chat up line began. He politely asked me where I came from and what I was doing out all on my own, gradually edging ever closer and pawing at me. He obviously wanted something more from me but when he finally overstepped the mark I clouted him one on the jaw. That quickly put an end to his 'hospitality' and found myself shoved out on to the street with only a few francs in my pocket.

Needing time to think this over I nipped into a bar near the railway station. I barely knew any French, just enough to be able to order a coffee. All around me men were being fondled by heavily made up women. Probably prostitutes I thought. A woman, whom I estimated to be around thirty to thirty-five years old was sitting on her own by the bar. She stood up and coming towards me asked in French whether I would like to go to bed with her. I looked at her blankly as this was beyond my linguistic capabilities and told her in German that I had not understood. To my surprise she then asked me in broken German what I was doing here. I told her I was just travelling through and looking for a job grape picking. We got talking some more and she bought me another coffee. When asked where I was sleeping that night I told her I planned to check out the local youth hostel but she kindly offered me a bed on her couch which I readily accepted.

She took me home to her nicely furnished two and a half room apartment and we talked some more until I began to feel tired. She then decided it was too much trouble to make up a bed on the couch, I could sleep with her as there was plenty space in her double bed. I had no objections, so I got washed first and then crawled in under the sheets. Half an hour later she came to bed and we fell asleep. Later on in the night though things hotted up. She started playing about with me and for the first time in my life I actually slept with a woman. I enjoyed being in such close contact with a woman who was older than me and seemed to care for me. Before long she taught me everything I ever needed to know about sex. We had a great time together.

My Introduction to Prostitution

She invited me to live with her. She was in fact only twenty-seven and she did not believe me when I told her I was also in my twenties and eventually she wormed it out of me that I was only seventeen. She admitted after a bit that she was a hooker because it was the fastest and easiest way to earn a comfortable living. At the time I believed that it was all for the best and could not see the harm in it. She went off in the evenings to ply her trade. Sometimes I accompanied her to the bar where she hung out. I cannot say it did not hurt me slightly that she could sleep with other men but because I knew it did not mean anything to her refused to let it bother me. At the same time I was learning fast about a completely different world to the one I was used to, for I was now living amongst the least reputable elements of society, prostitutes, pimps and johns. All the women were sexual temptresses and as a young and inexperienced lad I was drawn in by their promise of physical fulfilment. I knew I could learn a lot from them and I also found it easy to please them especially in bed. I learnt to adopt certain sexual practices, knowledge of which came in very useful in my later life as a pimp. My girlfriend always took a cheap hotel to do her tricks. She never brought any of her clients back to her flat. She had plenty of money to spare and handed it over whenever I needed anything whether it was clothes or just pocket money.

Life was good, if not even decadent. We often did not get up until the afternoon, then we got ready

Hallelujah Joe

to go out and eat, meet some friends and listen to music. We lived from day to day with no set plans. I was not her pimp although I was certainly learning the ropes. After seven months I knew enough for no one to pull the wool over my eyes or put one over on me. I understood by then how the whole red-light area ticked but I was soon to break off this cushy period in my life.

She cried when I left her. At first I had been a great new toy for her. Something she had managed to buy. But in time I had become much more important to her. She was genuinely very fond of me and perhaps even in love with me. From my side, she represented the love my mother could not give me. But it all changed the day my sister rang and triggered off the need in me to return. To this day I have not managed to find out how my sister managed to track me down. I had always got on well with Heide. Now she pleaded with me to return to Wuppertal because she had returned from East Germany to find our mother on her deathbed and I would have to be quick if I wanted to see her again before she died. It was a very difficult decision for me to take for I had broken probation. Here in France I was safe but if I set foot back in Germany I would be thrown back into jail like a shot. Nevertheless I took the next train to Strasbourg and across the border to Kehl. There I was hauled off the train because on checking my passport my name appeared on the wanted persons list.

Chapter Nine

MY MOTHER DIES

I was taken into police custody and brought back to Wuppertal to the same prison where I had done time in 1961. Once again I was all alone. I did not get to see my mother. Instead I was brought to court. I could not care less what happened to me. When asked whether I wanted to reapply for probation I immediately declined this offer without taking any legal advice because I just wanted to get it over and done with. I did not want to have a probation officer breathing down my neck. From there I was transferred to a judicial detention centre in Siegburg near Bonn. I was there approximately five weeks when my cell door opened and the prison clergyman stood before me. I was ordered to get up and dressed for my sister had just rung to say that my mother was in the throes of death and did I want to see her? I was shattered as this message was relayed to me but maintained my outward cool making out that I did not mind either way. The minister drove me to Wuppertal that night. He wanted to come to verify the truth of the story.

We arrived at the hospital and ran down the gleaming, polished corridors, breathing in the pervasive hospital smell that seems to be a blend of

Hallelujah Joe

disinfectant, blood and urine, until we reached the door of my mothers sick room. It suddenly hit me what my mother had said to me on the day of my confirmation. She said that I would arrive too late on the day she died and that I would not then be able to seek her forgiveness for all the problems I had caused her. I remembered retorting that she must be mad to even think of dying as she was only forty-four years old. But now only four years on here I stood outside the door of her deathbed. I could not shake this thought out of my head. It frightened me. I wanted to be able to speak to her and hear her pardon. When the door opened and I saw her lying there so helplessly under the crisp white sheets with tubes hanging out of her nose and conductors strapped to her veins as a drip slowly pumped fluid into her bloodstream, I could not hold myself back. I shouted out to her 'Mother!' At that she woke up. I rushed to her bedside. She lifted her eyelids and stared at me with wide open unseeing eyes and then she fell back into a coma.

She lived for another seventy-two hours but never regained consciousness. I spent a lot of time by her bedside. I sat with her without being able to speak to her. I was often alone with her when my brother and sister and new brother-in-law could not be there; mother and prodigal son. These hours seemed like an eternity and are engraved in my soul. They dug deep in to my inner recesses and chipped away at my cemented emotions. I was totally at odds with myself. I pleaded with God to make her well again.

My Mother Dies

But later as I watched her suffering increase and saw that she was just being kept alive artificially and in such pain I prayed to God that she might be left to die in peace. As I sat there watching her I imagined her dying there before me over and over again.

Her heart faltered and stopped beating for a while which seemed me like an eternity. Her face changed colour. Again and again I asked her to forgive me but there was no sign. Her forgiveness was not granted.

The fact that she was already dead I only realized when the nurse sent me and the other members of the family out of the room. Then she brought my mother's watch and jewellery to us in the corridor. We all stood transfixed until my brother stretched out and took these possessions and put them in his bag saying they were now his. The nurse came out again and whispered that we could go in and pay our last respects.

I went in first and beheld her corpse; all life had left her, only her body remained, or so it seemed to me. Her chin was held back in place by a bandage. It hit me then in a flash that I was now alone in the world. There was no one else to guide me. I looked over at my brother and even the could not overcome my hatred towards him. Then I glanced at my sister and felt nothing. I was like an empty shell, all feelings gone leaving only a cold exterior.

We drove home. My brother and sister discussed plans for the funeral but I did not get involved. A whole crowd of friends and relatives attended the

Hallelujah Joe

service and the actual burial. Again relatives whom I had never met before turned up. I heard them whispering behind my back about my being in prison, what a terrible child I had been and how I had no prospects. Furious I turned round and shouted at them to shut up. If they had been half as concerned earlier on when my mother needed them maybe she would still be alive today and not dead before her time. I got up and slipped away into a quiet corner of the chapel to be alone with my pain.

Chapter Ten

UNLUCKY IN LOVE

On the same day as the funeral I travelled back to prison in Sieburg. I never saw the minister again. But I was now a different person. I was asked if I wanted to train as a lathe operator. They wanted to give me a chance of finding a job and leading a normal life when I was released. I jumped at this offer and did the training. I even passed the exams with flying colours. Shortly afterwards I was set free and I returned to Wuppertal. My brother had decided to join the army. I too tried to enrol but was rejected on the grounds of my criminal record. I finally found work in the metal industry.

Around this time I met a girl. She came from Cologne, but her family was of East Prussian origin. She had an unusual, pretty name, Elsbetta. We spent every weekend together and it did not take me long to discover that she was deeply religious. She belonged to a Baptist church and to please her I went along to their church meetings. My heart was not really in it but I conformed and went through all the motions of praying, singing hymns and reading the Bible. All this failed to move me. I was only acting out the role of a pious Christian to win her affection.

Hallelujah Joe

One evening though it was a different story. We went along to a tent pitched in the Cologne-Mülheim district, not a beer tent but one for missionary work. It attracted quite a crowd, mainly believers, and we sat inside the tent on hard benches listening to various choirs of mixed musical ability. Towards the end of the evening, as was normally the case, there was a sermon and an invitation to all assembled to confess their sins and give up their lives to Jesus. This type of sermon was so completely different to those I had experienced in other churches to date. It was not so lofty, but offered practical advice bearing witness to everyday events. It did not wash over the top of you but seemed authoritative and directed specifically at you.

This evening was special, as I mentioned before. I felt that the preacher was talking directly to me, in fact he was really talking about me. What I craved was forgiveness, God's forgiveness. And Jesus can bring forgiveness because he chose to bear the sins of all mankind when he took up the cross and died for our sakes. Then the preacher shouted out to me, 'If you want a new start in this world then accept the life of Christ. Let him into your heart and he will change your life.' That night I was ready and willing to accept this message but first of all I wanted to wipe the slate clean with Elsbetta. She had to know I had been in prison. Until then I had been hiding this from her for I had not trusted in myself enough to tell her the truth about my past. Now the preacher had stated quite clearly that everyone

Unlucky in Love

without exception fails in the eyes of God, and everyone, no matter what crime he had committed, can ask for his forgiveness. So I was no longer afraid to let her know everything. I trusted in Elsbetta and her parents as Christians to understand. They would have been able to see that I had changed in the five months that they had known me.

Back at their house we were sitting in the living room when Elsbetta's mother asked me why I had become so quiet. She wondered if the speeches had made such an impact on me. I replied that I had been deeply moved and the time had come for me to make my pact with Jesus but I first wanted to speak to Elsbetta about it in private. We went up to her room and I told her the whole story. What I had done, the trial, the conviction and my term in prison. At first she sat silently and looked at me horrorstruck but at the end she took off her friendship ring which I had given her only a few weeks before and handed it back to me. She told me she could not go out with me and that was the end of it. She had nothing else to say. I left her house in a hurry without even saying goodbye to her parents.

I stopped on the steps of a new residential area for a moment and thought if these people who call themselves Christians do not give you a chance to change your life then just live your life the way it is. However bad they imagine you to be that is how you must be from now on, for you have been left no other choice. I had to fit in somewhere so I resolved then to lead a life of crime and no longer

Hallelujah Joe

strive towards idealistic goals of goodness and worthiness and finding beauty in this world. My heart was broken. I was now bent on revenge against everyone who had rejected me, Christians, my girlfriend, all women. I let my evil half take control over my soul. Instead of becoming a Christian that night I plunged into the grasp of Satan.

Chapter Eleven

A PIMP IN FRANKFURT

The decision made I lost no time in putting my new plans into action. The very next day I was on my way to Frankfurt to start off seriously on a life of crime. Now my earlier experiences of prostitution in France and my prison schooling in breaking and entering were put to good use. I knew how the red-light area went about its business on the basis of sex and power. And what really counted was that I had contacts, built up through life in prison where petty criminals learn all about the trade, everything from fraud and blackmarketeering to jobs involving violence.

From the main train station I headed straight towards the red-light area to a known bar where I knew there was a good chance of meeting up with some ex-prison mates. I was not disappointed for there propped up against the bar was a guy I knew from Siegburg. We had a few beers together and I soon found out all about what was going down on the scene there. Whilst we were talking I noticed a young woman on her own. She was not exactly pretty but that did not bother me. I asked my mate what the score was there and he told me she was on her own, her boyfriend was currently doing time.

Hallelujah Joe

So I asked her if she fancied a drink on me and paid her a few compliments, nothing too heavy, but we got talking and that night she invited me back to her place. Things turned out just like the last time in France. I became her new boyfriend and because I was used to the lifestyle I had no scruples about becoming dependent on her financially and putting her out to work on the game.

My friend introduced me to the Frankfurt criminal scene. When you are a new boy it is very important to make the right impression from the outset. Luckily I was given a good opportunity early on. I got into a spot of trouble in a snack bar. Without stopping to argue I hit out and the punch certainly hit its mark because the fellow toppled over. This won me the necessary respect from other hoodlums. I felt, however, that what I really lacked at that point in order to be properly kitted out was a weapon. So this was the first thing I bought myself out of the money my girlfriend earned through prostitution.

So I made a name for myself. Whenever I was asked where I came from I would reply from Holland. From my visits there I knew a smattering of Dutch. And when asked my name I called myself Joe, for I thought this would help keep the police off my tracks. And so I became 'Dutch Joe', an instantly recognizable name in the Frankfurt underworld.

I was a keen football fan but it so happened that I got exceeding drunk at a European cup final match

A Pimp in Frankfurt

in Amsterdam and started brawling with two Dutch policemen. I chucked them both into the canal. Reinforcements soon stormed in and beat the brains out of me. I was sentenced to ten weeks imprisonment but I used this time fruitfully by buying a language course and one of the guards helped me learn Dutch.

Amongst pimps you must understand that there are different rankings. Two bit Charleys and male tarts were on the bottom rung. These guys really had problems and used to hang around the station taking on the real dregs of society. The wise guys in the business who made big bucks out of their girls moved in up town circles and lived in the best areas. I soon got to know who they were and I shared their sense of class.

Most prostitution took place in the respectable suburb of Sachsenhausen, in a huge block of flats. Usually the pimp rented out two flats, one immediately above the other. The girlfriend entertained in the lower flat whilst the boyfriend was always upstairs if required for her protection. At one time I had three or four girls working for me without making my life too complicated. I could go about with them and mix with all sorts, even the real tough squad. But I never ever hit one of these women. I found this unworthy of a man and even in breach of the unwritten code of criminal conduct. I will say this even if it does sound presumptuous for it is the truth. The women who worked for me chose to be prostitutes. No one ever forced their hand.

Hallelujah Joe

Most of them fell off the straight and narrow because of some major disappointment in their lives, or even through sheer loneliness. Through the promise of love they were gradually drawn to the streets for the first time. Most of them were simple girls but there were exceptions to this rule. Eva, for example, was a former law student, and daughter of the local district court judge. She hated her father because he had once sexually abused her, and she never managed to get over this. She became a feminist lesbian with a live-in girlfriend.

The pimp's job is to see to it that his girls pass over their total cash. He controls everything and drives around collecting the illicit earnings. Often pimps discuss amongst themselves who controls what, where and when. The money pays for the apartments, hairdressing, food and so on. The balance belongs to the pimp. During the day everyone rests to keep fit for the night's activities. I used to go walking, meet up with some others or perhaps go to a football match or boxing event. As I mentioned earlier, I often travelled to some of the big matches but usually in a big drinking party. We would get tanked up and so stinking drunk that we actually never saw anything of the game.

After one such game, I think it was Bayern Munich against Ajax Amsterdam, I was so inebriated that I was seeing double but I still insisted on driving back. I stuck a plaster over one eye and raced up the motorway at top speed all the way from Munich to Frankfurt.

A Pimp in Frankfurt

Financially things were going well for me thanks to the girls. I was always smartly dressed and drove the very latest sports cars available.

There were also a lot of crazy people who were pimps. One called himself the 'Emperor of China' and drove a four-wheeled chariot through the station backstreets to cash up. Or Tornado Joe. His speciality was taking care of the street gas lamps by taking pot shots at them. Mostly any fighting was taken care of with our fists and I was always quick off the mark in that respect. One evening I was standing with one of my girls in a restaurant when a drunk came in squinting at our teacups. He looked sideways at the girl and calling her an old bat proceeded to spit in her tea.

I hit the roof. Afterwards they told me that I had almost beaten him senseless, punching him all the way out of the restaurant and four hundred yards down the street to almost in front of the station. There I intended to throw him under a tram but I finally came to my senses. It was a very bad situation. I simply lost my head and went totally berserk and I was shocked by my own brutality.

The real people who pull the strings in the red-light area are the pimps or else the gentlemen of hidden identity behind the organized crime rings. These men are never seen in the area but send in their henchmen and employ licensees to operate their sex and criminal enterprises. In those days the gangs we hear of nowadays had not yet found a footing although towards the end of my time in Frankfurt

Hallelujah Joe

a sort of German-Italian mafia was emerging. They later went into business but were busted by a special police commission. There were also various pimp wars between Moroccans and Yugoslavians which spread as far afield as Berlin and they were even known to shoot each other.

I was never afraid because I did not care what happened to me. There was no one in my life to shed any tears if I were to die suddenly. I knew there was something lacking in me, a terrible void. I knew also that in my line of work you had to be strong to survive so I tried to fill the void and find strength by drowning myself in alcohol. Before arriving in Frankfurt I had hardly drunk at all but I soon learned for there were only two ways of proving that you were a real man there. Firstly you had to be able to fight which I ably demonstrated. I still have the scars from these scraps and can even show the marks where someone smashed a broken beer glass into my face. Secondly, you had to be able to hold a good drink. I learned to down the stuff and stay *compos mentis* but I could not stop myself from becoming addicted. It got so bad that after a few years I needed two bottles of vodka every morning in order to function normally. Finally I reached the point where I would crawl to the fridge to fetch the bottle of vodka and stick the neck down my throat. Most of the first bottle was spilled as my hands used to shake so much. Only then could I sit behind the steering wheel of my car.

The one thing that really used to get on my nerves

A Pimp in Frankfurt

at that time was when Christians used to come to the station to sing their songs and try to convert people into believing in Jesus. Or when a sister from The Salvation Army came into the bar where I was with her collection box. I could not stand the sight of this. Anything to do with Christianity got my temper up and unleashed my hatred towards them. For it always brought back to mind what had happened between Elsbetta and myself that fateful evening in Cologne. I could not get over the fact that these people had something special, something that was so very important to them in their lives. Otherwise they would not dare venture into this area and let themselves be made a laughing stock. I could not have borne to be treated in this fashion. They allowed themselves to be virtually crucified and were the brunt of the most vitriolic abuse. I was one of their worst opponents and regularly took them on, trying to make them feel as small as possible.

In my mind The Salvation Army was an organization for loonies with a religious leaning. They were only there as the very last resort for people who had no one else to turn to and nobody to help them when they were left with nothing. Only when you were destitute could you go to The Salvation Army and get a bowl of soup from them. I thought this was their sole purpose as an organization.

Once a young female Salvation Army worker came into the bar where I was drinking along with some of my mates. As a joke I stuck 10 marks into

Hallelujah Joe

her box and told her it was for my pillow in heaven and I asked her to pray for me. She quick-wittedly replied that it was a pity she did not have a key for the collection box to give me my money back because I could get the pillow for free for no one has to buy his way into the kingdom of heaven.

Chapter Twelve

DOING TIME

Crime was the only life I knew and because crime does not pay it is not surprising that I was constantly behind bars. All in all I spent nine and a half years in prison in the thirteen years between 1962 until my final release in 1975. So for the vast majority of time I was stuck in the slammer. One prison sentence stretched into the next. I was found guilty of armed robbery, theft, pimping, grievous bodily harm, driving without a licence. And on the pronouncement of each sentence I became more and more a hopeless case in the eyes of the judiciary. I was treated as a hardened criminal and so there was no question of trying to rehabilitate me into society. It boiled down to just dealing out the proper punishment. The threat of imprisonment had lost its restraining effect because I was just as much at home in that environment as outside. It did not matter to me whether I was inside or out or what became of me because nobody cared a fig for me anyway.

I felt like this not only because of my past bad experiences with my mother who never visited me in prison or the girl in Cologne who had left me in the lurch. No, it was also because in prison you are

Hallelujah Joe

treated more like a number than a person. You are always referred to by your prison number and the number of years you are currently serving. Because I had been caught up in the penal system from a very early age over the years I became so habituated to life inside that a three-year sentence meant next to nothing to me, nor to other seasoned inmates. We had almost got used to the monotony of the daily routine, but I stress 'almost' for you never fully overcome it. At times I reached an all-time low of depression and I was not the only prisoner to suffer from these intense lows.

Distractions were needed to take our minds off such things. I had always been quite a creative person so as one of the longer standing inmates I managed to get into the writing guild and became editor of the prison newspaper. The main editorial objective was to bring about minor improvements in the quality of prison life. Some complaints were levelled at the disgusting quality of prison food, others at the ridiculously low levels of leisure opportunities available and there was always mention of introducing parole. This was the early seventies, a time of major reforms even in the penal system. Emphasis was now to be placed on rehabilitation and the prisoner's reintroduction into normal society instead of the old punishment, penance and repentance syndrome or short sharp shock system.

It was not only a prime time for political reform for the seventies also heralded a resurgence of Christianity. The Jesus squad movement swept

Doing Time

across the Atlantic from America into Europe and also flooded into Germany. Its supporters were young and enthusiastic people, descendants of the hippy generation of the sixties and they were drawn to Jesus in much the same way as the generation before were drawn to flowerpower and smoking pot. They sang modern songs to guitar accompaniment and were possessed by a limitless religious fervour. So it was no wonder that prisons were an obvious target for their conversion attempts.

As a general rule they used to come on Sundays to church services and sing their 'Jesus Loves You' tunes. Because of my past experience I still only felt scorn and resentment towards them. I continued to play my tricks on them to test whether their love was genuine mainly just to prove to myself that they were really only hypocrites of the worst variety.

Once I asked the leader of one of these groups quite bluntly whether if he managed to find a convert within the prison confines, which was indeed his ultimate purpose here, would he invite that person to his home? He hummed and hawed giving the excuse that he was newly married and had a six-month-old baby. I swore at him and told him he had no doubt been asleep during the sermons for he evidently did not understand the message of God. He had just shown his true colours and was indeed a hypocrite. And just to make him feel worse I told him not to worry for I had had no intention of paying him a visit. He started to stutter reaffirming that he would not take anybody in on principle. I for one

Hallelujah Joe

should know what prisoners were like. I just looked at him and thought here was another typical Christian. They come and sing and spout mighty words but they are not prepared to take any consequences. Their message is hollow.

I much preferred the company of a more honest woman. Jutta was not religious but in charge of a classics organization in Frankfurt and she was a true idealist. She believed in the inherent goodness of mankind. Regardless of what forces of evil drive a person, she believed there was still a spark of goodness in everyone. Of this she was totally convinced. And what is more she was prepared to do something about it, get involved. She cared about people whom nobody else cared tuppence about and Joe Scharwächter fitted this bill to a tee.

She visited me, talked to me, was concerned for my welfare and generally propped me up. She encouraged me to do something to stop myself from rotting away, and pointed out the lousy conditions of other prisoners in my block, especially those of the foreigners. They could scarcely speak any German and were completely at the mercy of the authorities and lawyers. She tried to persuade me to help them because she knew I was one of the few people there who could.

At first I rebelled against this idea. I had a few unpleasant racial terms for foreigners who were commonly regarded as the scum of German society. I could not care a toss what happened to them. But I thought it over and became enlightened, just as

Doing Time

Jutta had said I would. When I spoke to some of them it soon became apparent that they were given a really tough time. They were cast aside and stamped upon. With my arm-long criminal record and corresponding legal knowledge I knew for certain something was amiss, and I could help. I could give them pointers, write letters for them and such like. I got stuck in and soon I was a walking authority on penal law. I discovered that certain people who had not committed any crime were wrongfully being imprisoned on the basis of unfounded suspicion. I also witnessed the release of some innocent victims through proper mediation with the legal authorities.

Because of my involvement in this area I was elected as the first prisoner representative for over 600 inmates on the Frankfurt-Prengesheim prison investigative committee. As you will find out later, the last time I had made an appearance in this district courtroom, the judge put me down for three years and nine months sentence. The prosecuting attorney, a real swine in my opinion, addressed me saying that if he noticed any change in my behaviour he would be the first to help me try to overcome my past. At the time I did not take him at his word.

Chapter Thirteen

SHALL I BE YOUR PROSTITUTE?

My last prison stint was passed yet again in Butzbach. I knew every inch of that prison. Again I took over control of the prison newspaper and everything fell back into place as if I had never been away. Sporadically, in a blue period, I felt a calling to improve my life, at least to get it organized. Like many of the inmates I thought the answer and the road to improvement might lie in finding myself a good wife.

But for me the problem ran deeper for I understood it was inherently linked with my inability to relate properly with women. I had never had a normal relationship with my mother or girlfriends and I had never married. I knew how to handle women. I could flatter them and pay them compliments and please them in bed but at the same time I made them subservient. I used them and exercised my authority over them all; tricks I had learned pimping. But I could not bring myself to let any woman love the person inside me. I did not even know myself whether I was indeed capable of love.

Nevertheless the question of how I was going to

Shall I Be Your Prostitute?

find myself a good wife was never far from my mind. Some people wrote to the daily newspapers. I thought I would try the radio network. I wrote to Radio Luxembourg the following snippet: 'Prisoner seeks lady friend. Marriage considered.' I thought I might get one or two replies at the most for what respectable woman would want to correspond with a prisoner?

The response was extraordinary. I was bowled over by the fact that I received seventy-seven letters in a single week. Were women that daft that they would consider marrying me? After all they did not know a thing about me. All they knew was that I was in prison. There had to be something a bit dodgy.

But I read every single letter of the seventy-seven. I especially liked two of them. The first was from a seventy-seven-year-old woman who wrote that she was too old to get married but if I wanted I could take advantage of her life's experiences to date. She would be very happy if I replied and we could write to each other regularly. I was very touched for I realized it must take a very special kind of woman with a big heart to listen to a young people's radio programme and respond so openly through the generation gap. I did write to her and we became good friends. It was only later she told me she was a Christian. There had been no mention of this in her first letter.

The second letter of interest, written by a young woman from Niederrhein, was more in keeping with

Hallelujah Joe

the original aim of the exercise. We wrote to one another for a few months and discovered that we had a lot in common and a mutual liking developed. I did not hide anything from her in my letters. I told her exactly who I was and what I had done, that I had been a pimp even. I did not hold anything back. She did not seem to mind. Everything was great, and what was even more fantastic was that I had some parole coming up for the first time ever. I thanked the aforementioned penal reforms for this good fortune.

On the train to Krefeld with trembling knees and clutching a bouquet of flowers I kept turning over in my mind how she would look, how she would react when she saw me. Was this the breakthrough I was looking for, the beginning of a happy, normal life, with possible family. Maybe this was all I had ever wanted.

I hurried from the train through the station to our meeting place and even ran towards her when I caught sight of her standing there waving. She was as pretty as a picture. I took her in my arms, spun her around and thought this is it. Here at last is a real woman, the one for me. But then she asked me, 'Do you want me to go to work for you?'

Chapter Fourteen

DEFLATED AND DESPONDENT

I was devastated that the woman I had contemplated marrying to start off on a new life together could offer to prostitute herself for my sake. I could not believe I had heard correctly and asked her if she was serious. When she assured me she was I turned on my heel leaving her standing and spent all my available money on alcohol. I travelled back to Frankfurt and drank nonstop for two days solid. I was meant to report back to prison then but I could not face it. I thought it did not matter what happened to me now that I was out. I would face the consequences later if I ever got caught. In the meantime I would head off to Rotterdam and start a new career there. As far as I was concerned the prosecuting attorney could finish off the rest of my sentence for me with a razor-blade up his bottom. It could be his problem not mine from now on.

Then I remembered Jutta, the woman from the classics organization who had done so much for me and had never forsaken me in times of need. I could not disappoint her. So I rang her up shortly before midnight and told her I could not go back to prison. I could see no point in it. I was going to Rotterdam. She asked me where I was but I was not going to

Hallelujah Joe

fall into that easy trap and let her pass on to the police which bar I was in so that they could pick me up. I simply thanked her for all she had done for me, put down the receiver and carried on drinking.

A few hours later there was a tap on my shoulder. I turned round to face Jutta who ordered me to drink up for she had to talk to me. This woman had done what no other woman had ever done for me. She had come out looking for me not for any sexual gratification but because she still believed in me, and she believed that goodness could prevail. I could not fight her. I drank up quietly and went with her.

She naturally told me I had to go back to Butzbach. I hotly refused but what were my alternatives? We tried finding a hotel but it was 3.30 a.m. and they were all shut. So I suggested knocking up the prison minister. Jutta was not so sure he would help but I said he ought to practise what he preached every Sunday from the pulpit. Inwardly, however, I was convinced that he would do exactly the opposite for he was a Christian was he not and therefore a hypocrite like all the other Christians I had put to the test. At the very most he would tell me to come again the following day when I had sobered up, showered and made myself respectable. Yes, he would advise me to come during his consultation hours and talk about it then.

I was therefore very surprised when I rang the bell at Minister Hermann Lübke's house to find that he answered the door at 4 o'clock in the morning and

Deflated and Despondent

recognizing me invited me in although I stank of sweat, booze and all sorts of unpleasant odours. Jutta disappeared quickly. I had made a big enough mess in her car as it was.

That night I experienced for the first time spiritual welfare at work. The minister listened to me patiently and did not try to offer inane advice after just five minutes. For four hours he paid close attention whilst I smoked four packets of cigarettes and spilled my heart out to him. For the first time ever I could really talk to someone, disclose my whole past and explain how exactly I felt about myself. We also talked about Jesus but there was no pressure exerted for me to come down in favour of Christianity.

Finally I was allowed to go and wash and my clothes were taken away to be cleaned. I slept on the couch in Lübke's office.

I woke up feeling a thousand times lighter. I had thought earlier that day that nobody believed in me, nobody would give me a chance and now two people had proved me wrong. I got over the disappointment of the woman from Krefeld and plucked up renewed courage. By the following afternoon I had reported back to prison. My return caused a minor sensation. Of course I told a pack lies, laying it on thick about what a great time I had had on the outside with my new woman.

Chapter Fifteen

MY DREAM WOMAN

I was working on the prison newspaper when Minister Lübke came into the editorial office to tell me that a group of young Christians was soon going to pay us a visit and perhaps I could write an article. I felt quite sick at the thought and made no attempt to hide my adverse feelings towards Christians. But the minister forced the issue and urged me to write something as it was bound to be a bonus.

I was therefore dead set against this group when they arrived at Buchwald one Saturday. All the same I went up to them and surprisingly I immediately softened when my ears picked up a definite Dutch twang. For I had been born in Holland and had not completed an intensive Dutch course in prison for nothing.

I chatted to one of the girls in Dutch. During this conversation I glanced to my left and I was completely bowled over. There sat my ideal woman just as I had always imagined her: blonde, blue-eyed with a slim shapely figure. My mind was obsessed by a single question: How could I lay my hands on her?

I walked towards her wanting to introduce myself but not knowing quite how to go about it. The right

My Dream Woman

words escaped me. She sat there watching me approach and then I blurted out the first thing that sprung to mind and asked her if she wanted to go to bed with me. I immediately went beetroot but she on the other hand maintained her cool and replied that she did not feel any need for that. I asked her how old she was and then questioned why she was not interested in men if she was indeed twenty-two. I was astounded by her reply for she said she was waiting for the right man that God was going to send her. I tried to laugh it off insisting that you had to try it out first before you snare the right person.

But deep down her reply had a profound effect on me. There had to be something very special involved when such a good looking woman relied so heavily on God. We talked for a long time. Later I tried to find out her address. After talking to the leader of the group I was permitted to have it. Her name was Doris and she worked as a governess in Bad Nauheim.

Chapter Sixteen

MY CONVERSION

That very same evening we met, on 27 June 1974, I wrote to my dream woman for the first time. Another first that day was to pick up a Christian newspaper. In it I had read an article about a sixteen-year-old boy who had broken into a chemist's and run away from home. On Christmas Eve he was standing by the side of the road waiting for a lift to take him anywhere when a lorry driver spotted him and taking pity on the young lad brought him home with him to celebrate Christmas with his family. He was concerned that he was not at his own home unwrapping his Christmas presents like every other kid of his age should. That night that sixteen-year-old learnt two different kinds of experiences. First of all that there is forgiveness in this world for he telephoned the chemist whom he had robbed and his misconduct was pardoned. Also later his sentence was reduced to probation. But far more importantly he learned about the forgiveness of God.

When I read this article I was transported back in time to the missionary tent and I knew then that I was being given a second chance to choose which path I wanted to take. I got down off my stool and on to my knees on the floor of my cell and I prayed.

My Conversion

In my prayer I told God that I was not sure whether he existed but I knew that he was not an old man in a white beard who hovered above the whole world. I asked him that if he did exist and the millions of his Christian followers were not lying, to come into my life then and make of it whatever he willed. And suddenly from one second to the next I knew he existed. I felt afraid, an emotion I had shut off a long time ago. Now I was afraid of the consequences of being a Christian. If I was to walk with Christ then my life had to change. It could not go on as it had in the past.

Chapter Seventeen

THE FINAL CONSEQUENCE

Other converts starting off a new life in Christ often recount that they are gripped by an overpowering sense of joy. For me the greatest feeling was one of immense relief. My guilt at the errors of my ways and the evil I had inflicted on others was lifted like a ton weight from my soul. All the hate that I had stored up in life, the derision I felt for certain people, all the feelings of revenge were lifted from me. I, Joachim Scharwächter, the professional criminal and sinner, was suddenly freed from inner torment. God was by my side and would bring order into my screwed-up life.

Exactly for this reason I felt not only joy but also terror for it was clear to me that if God now had the final say in my life and not as before the evil side in me then I could no longer do the things I was used to do and I was terribly afraid of making such a complete change and taking this gigantic step into the unknown.

Although it sounds crazy at least I was someone in the criminal circle. I had a reputation to lose, even if it was a doubtful one. Dutch Joe, a converted Christian! None of my mates would believe it. Possibly they would see it as a betrayal and traitors

The Final Consequence

were punished according to criminal ethics. I would cease to exist and be blotted out completely as a person to them.

So for three months I told nobody about my change in faith except Minister Lübke and my girlfriend, Doris. Around this three-month stage an evangelical meeting with a Hungarian missionary Ladislav Barony was arranged for the prison. This was to comprise of a series of speeches and sermons advertising for new Christian converts to step forward. You could get spiritual counselling, confess your sins and bring your corrupted life back into harmony. It was in other words to be a mission.

Now I knew the day had dawned and I now had to freely admit in front of everyone that I had taken up the life of Jesus. The minister came again to ask me if I would write an article for the prison paper. This was my opportunity to let everyone know what a child of God I had become. I prayed and entitled the article 'The Final Consequence'. A week later every one of the 720 inmates knew.

All hell was let loose. I knew only a few at most would understand. The majority looked on it as a desertion and took their revenge by hanging me over the balustrade. They awaited the right moment to make me pay for my actions in the past. Before I had had the squeeze on them and made them do things against their will. Now they would get their own back and let all their hatred of me out. I could no longer protect myself physically because use of violence was not Christian-like behaviour. An inmate can always tell a Christian through his actions sometimes even better than the Christian knows himself.

I prepared myself mentally to withstand any punishment given. That was the only way to prove that I was indeed a true Christian. In reality I still felt very much alone and defenceless. I only had the minister, my girlfriend and the evangelists. And Jesus too, of course. In him I regularly confided my troubles through prayer. At first these conversations were the only prop I had to sustain my faith until I received a Bible and a correspondence course to further my religious education.

Chapter Eighteen

DOES SHE LOVE ME?

I stayed in regular close contact with Doris. One day I bombarded her with an outrageous request. A fellow prisoner who worked with me on the editorial team of the newspaper had to travel to Düsseldorf to sort out a few things from his past. He did not know how he was going to get there so I wrote to Doris and asked her to drive him there and back. She did so readily because this was first nature to her but as a consequence she got into terrible trouble with her brother-in-law who severely reprimanded her for travelling about the country with a convicted prisoner. Anything could have happened according to him. When I heard this accusation I flew into a rage at the man and promptly sat down to write him a strong letter. How dare he make such implications . . . I even threatened him with violence.

But on writing this down I suddenly realized that I was more than fond of Doris, I was actually in love with her. Everything about her assumed primary importance as far as I was concerned — her purity of spirit, her virginity, her naturalness. Before these were distant qualities and now very dear to my heart. She had melted my resistance and now I wanted to protect her, to love and cherish her. I understood

Hallelujah Joe

then why I was so up in arms against her brother-in-law and wanted to beat him. It was because I loved her.

So what was I do about it now that I had come to this realization? The only thing possible was to write to her. I told her all about my newly discovered feelings for her and declared my love asking for her hand in marriage. I had to know for sure what she felt about me.

The following days were agony as I awaited her reply. I was tossed between hope and despair, expectation and rejection. I counted every minute of each passing day. In principle everything was against me. She was a young Christian with strong principles with a promising life in front of her, and I despite my new-found faith was a prisoner with a long list of convictions behind me and no specific job training. I had a whole misspent past to overcome.

Finally after seven days I held in my hand the letter I craved, but I could scarcely bear to open it, turning it backwards and forwards through my fingers. My heart was in my mouth. She wrote yes she wanted to become my wife. She thought I was the man God had intended for her.

What I did not know at that time was that she did not like having to make this decision. She thought it over very carefully and spoke about it to Pastor Baranyi. He was the only one who encouraged her to take this step. This old man who had so much experience of prisoners and their

Does She Love Me?

infinite capacity for doing the dirty told her to go ahead for he honestly believed that Jesus had changed me, and quoted the biblical saying 'the old is gone, look, all is now new'. He advised her that it would not be easy but she could marry me.

Chapter Nineteen

TURNED DOWN AND TAKEN ON

That Doris said yes to a future with me which was bound to be beset with problems was astonishing enough. But there was another more serious matter with which to contend. How would her parents react. They would probably recommend that I first find a job and maybe then after three years I might be granted permission to go out with their daughter. It was not long before I received a letter from them. It started off, 'Dear Joachim'. I really wanted to lay the letter aside at that point because that was how my mother had always addressed me whenever I had eaten something I should not have touched and then there was always a fight.

But I continued reading it through. In the middle of it there was a key sentence which I will quote here, 'If Jesus has forgiven your sins, then we have no right to condemn you', and they signed the letter 'best wishes from your loving parents'. For me this had an even greater impact on me than my forthcoming marriage for I had never had proper parents. I never knew my father and this greeting from my future in-laws moved me to tears. This was the first time I had cried for over fifteen years.

I took the letter and showed it to the prison

Turned Down and Taken On

director and asked him what he thought of it. He admitted he had been in the prison for twenty years and he had never read anything like it. He thought it quite fantastic. I got on very well with this man and was very upset to hear a few weeks after my release that he was shot in prison whilst being taken hostage. He had given himself up to the hostage-takers in exchange for a female social worker. It was him who had awarded me parole so that I could journey to meet my new parents. Everyone worked towards my rehabilitation, even the Frankfurt prosecuting attorney. He kept his word that he had given at my last court hearing.

On 7 March 1975 we were married in a registry office in Bad Nauheim and again in the Free Evangelical church in Witten. My parents-in-law belonged to this church community and there I was openly accepted by everyone. I was greeted as a friend by total strangers because I was one of Christ's faithful.

Only my own family rejected me saying that I had switched from one extreme to another. Instead of being incredibly angry I had just changed to being super pious. Both stances were totally incomprehensible to them.

Chapter Twenty

BREAKING WITH THE PAST

Whoever starts afresh in life must break with his or her past. This is a very important point especially for people like myself who would like nothing better than to be able to bury the past. It sounds self-evident and just a matter of common sense but it is in fact a very difficult thing to accomplish and it is also very rarely achieved. Where most people fall down is in trying to bridge the gap between past and future. They are afraid of taking the leap forward in one go and venturing into completely unfamiliar territory so they think they can do it in gradual stages but they cannot. Before long they are back exactly where they started and living their lives of old.

I was different. From the outset I was resolved to make a clean break of it and told everyone my intentions. I used a day's parole to travel up to Frankfurt to set the records straight with former buddies. I told them I did not want a single penny of the money they owed me, all I wanted was to be left in peace. From now on we were square and no one was to blame for the parting of our ways. They knew I would not grass on them ever or let out any of the trade secrets for there is honour

Breaking with the Past

amongst thieves. None of them actually believed I would stick at my new lifestyle. It had been tough telling them but it did have an immediate positive effect. I had burnt my bridges and I felt even closer to God.

The biggest unchanging problem in my life now was my drinking. I admitted was an alcoholic and needed a few bottles of spirits a day. Even in prison I had managed to feed this addiction for drink and my conversion to Christianity had not helped me break the habit. Perhaps I now drunk less but I was still hooked on it. As long as you had money in prison you could easily come by alcohol and even if you ran out of hard cash there were all sort of methods of brewing your own lethal concoctions from next to anything, such as aftershave.

My wife did not seem to notice and therefore had no idea of the extent to which I drank. The day we were in Frankfurt breaking with my past we were sitting in one of the criminal bars for over an hour and a half. When I stood up to leave my wife pointed out that I still had to finish my drink. I picked up my pint and was about to tip the glass back when I noticed that it was still nearly full. I had only taken a few mouthfuls from this single pint in all the time I had been perched there at the bar. I heard myself announce to God there and then in front of everyone that if I only needed to drink that little in that time then I never needed to touch a drop again. I put the beer glass down and to this day I have never picked

Hallelujah Joe

one up again. I never had any withdrawal symptoms or indeed had any urge to take up drinking again. I do not even take an occasional beer.

But smoking was a lot more difficult to give up. It took me years to stop.

Chapter Twenty-one

A NEW START IN FREEDOM

On 15 September 1975 I was released from prison early and in my pocket I had a letter dated 1 September with a job offer from a company in Bochum. My wife therefore gave up her job in Bad Nauheim and moved to Witten. On my first day of freedom I very nearly ended up in prison again. That morning at 7 o'clock the prison gates slammed behind me and my wife was outside to pick me up. Together we drove to Bochum and arrived at my future offices at around 11 o'clock. As soon as he met me the boss started shouting at me in a flaming temper asking me what the point was of turning up now when I should have been there on the first. Where had I been all this time and to add even more insult to injury he accused me of being off on a drunken bender for the fortnight. I felt my anger rising and my blood beginning to boil. I pushed his desk towards him to pin him back against the wall. But my wife stopped me from doing anything telling me not to bother as we would look elsewhere. I did not want to argue with my wife on my first day out so we left. Back in the car she suggested that we drive to the steelworks. I admit I thought she was acting crazy for I had already applied some time ago for

Hallelujah Joe

work there and was told that they were not taking on any more people fullstop because of the crisis in the industry. But what was the use of going against the wishes of a mad saint?

In the office section of the steelworks I was given an interview by the Personnel Officer, Mr Braun. I told him I had just been released from prison and he asked me to come back in a fortnight and he would try to sort something out. I signed up for unemployment benefit at the social security office and then went home pleased that I had two weeks in which to find my feet. After one week I drove back to prison to help a friend in need. That was the start of my prison counselling service which I later continued with the Frankfurt Christian support organization *Notwende* (Emergency). A fortnight later I kept my appointment with Mr Braun. He knew I had trained as a metal worker but he asked if I would mind switching to engineering. I naturally asked how much the job would pay for I now had a wife to look after and she was now unemployed. He estimated between eight marks twenty-seven pfennigs to nine marks twenty-seven pfennigs, probably 8,27 to start off with. I agreed because really the wage was much less important than finding work where the employer actually knew my past but was still prepared to take me on board.

I started immediately on a six weeks' trial training under the Chief Engineer who was to be my new boss. He looked me up and down and said I looked a man worthy of respect. I agreed with him but

A New Start in Freedom

wondered straight away how much he knew about me. He took me down to the compressor chambers and explained the whole works. Within six weeks I was responsible for the whole gas, water and oil maintenance for the factory.

The Chief Engineer meant what he said about me and recommended that I be given the top wage for an engineer which was over eleven marks. I would have been happy to work for eight and now I was earning a mini fortune, taking in over 2000 marks a month, including danger money, night shift and double-time for working on Sundays. It was a lot of money, especially back in 1975. The first time I brought my pay packet home to my wife I cried, for it was the first honest money I had ever earned as an adult.

Chapter Twenty-two

JOIN THE SALVATION ARMY? NOT A CHANCE!

So I slaved away in the steelworks. It was dirty and hot and a hard graft especially for someone like me who had never known regular work. But I struggled on and made the most of it. The best part as I already mentioned was earning my own money and not through exploiting women.

I did ten days shift then I had four days off. That gave me time to look after the social welfare of people in prison, to talk to them and offer assistance where possible. In just under three years I had travelled over 200,000 kilometres from one prison to another. I started off with the action group 'Emergency' and helped build it up. It was basically a letter answering service, operating a bit like a problem page. People wrote to us with their worries and were replied to anonymously. This was designed to protect the people working for the organization from any reprisals. My wife and I also lectured and gave Bible lessons in the prisons. It was important not to come over as being naive in this sort of environment. I have always tried to avoid involving young, idealistic people who had led cushioned lives

Join the Salvation Army? Not a Chance!

even if it was just to bring them along to join in the singing. They had to be aware that they were dealing with devious men and women and they also had to be strong so as not to waiver when put to the test. For instance, they had to be prepared to take someone home if requested or perhaps help that person find work.

We were given tremendous support from our parish and I think we also put back a little bit into the community. There was a sort of stuffy intellectual aura about church itself when I first started attending. I was not a man to mince my words and therefore was not afraid to unmask a few faults where I thought there was room for improvement. In any case I got the parish heated up on the subject of extra church activities and made them think afresh on certain set conventions. To cite an example, it seemed inconceivable for the church to celebrate communion without holy wine but because I was a reformed alcoholic this topic was given a lengthy airing. Opinions varied. Some people thought that those in the congregation suffering from alcohol related problems should sit at the front and be given grape juice instead. I spoke quite vehemently against this motion as I was opposed to such segregation and open discrimination and won the argument.

I assure you it is not easy for someone who has given up drink to mix with people with normal drinking habits without feeling antisocial. At work it was quite common to invite a group of fellow workers to celebrate over a few glasses with you on

Hallelujah Joe

some occasion or other. But how could I join in and take my turn? I did not want to feel excluded or inhospitable. To help find the solution my wife and I sought advice from the Blue Cross Temperance League who were able to give us a wealth of information on how to cope with alcoholism and readjust to social pressures. Our advisor suggested that the problem of standing one's hand at work could be solved by offering them a pint of milk each instead of alcohol. It was an odd idea and at first I was rather taken aback by it but I came round to his way of thinking. My wife thought milk was too little on its own to offer so she arranged to cook everyone a cutlet in addition. I was the first person ever in the history of the steelworks to dole out milk coupled with a cutlet instead of booze. Word of this unusual event spread like wildfire and lots of fellow workers wanted to understand why I did not drink. I explained that through alcohol I had hit rock bottom and I was now happy to be free of the affliction. I could fully understand the urge in others to drink but I was no longer prepared to buy anyone a drink because I knew where it could lead.

Quite a number of people at work with drink problems came to speak to me. One colleague followed me about for weeks holding out a bottle of beer for me and taunting me to take a drink until one day I found him drunk and incapable on the tram line in the steelworks. I chucked him fully clothed under a cold shower until he came round and sobered up so that he would not be given the sack on the spot.

Join the Salvation Army! Not a Chance!

After that I became the representative at work for alcohol-related incidents mainly because I stood out as a prize example that it was not impossible to work in a steel factory and not drink.

In May 1979 my wife and I were siting one evening in front of the television. On the main TV channel there was an Elvis Presley film 'Flaming Star' and on the other side there was a documentary entitled 'Jesus in St Pauli'. I have always been a great Elvis fan and had been looking forward to seeing his film on the television but my wife insisted on seeing the documentary. I did not like giving in to her but now and again any wife deserves to have a little of her own way so I relented and we watched the documentary on The Salvation Army's work in St Pauli, the red-light area in Hamburg.

At the end of the programme I was completely shattered. I had watched young, naive Christians put themselves into an exceedingly dangerous environment and set up a prayer circle in the struggle to win converts. I was transported back to my past for I knew so well that world that they were trying to conquer. These people with such little inkling about the downtown life and criminal activities dared to enter it whilst I sat safe at home in front of the television when I was the very one that could help them with their challenge.

My wife was also in a state of shock after the documentary and she said that she was now convinced that was the place God wanted us to work. I tried hard to deny it, anything else but not

Hallelujah Joe

The Salvation Army. I could not imagine myself actually wearing their uniform or standing in the street in it with a bunch of old ladies singing 'Jesus Loves You'. But inwardly I had known for a long time that God wanted me in his full-time service. I understood that the present was merely a trial period to prove that I could earn a living and support my wife. If you become a Christian whilst in prison it is more important on your release to be able to say that you have slogged your guts out at work with God's blessing than to say you were sent to Bible school at the prison director's instigation and emerged as a minister. You feel you have to stand on your own two feet and not be over protected by the church. I felt fine in myself and proud of my own progress until I watched this documentary.

I fought against my destiny but I was already held tightly in its grip. We took a trip to the Dortmund office on the pretext of going there only to find out more about the social work undertaken by The Salvation Army. The branch was directed by a Dutchman, Major Eddie Pauwel. Of all the nationalities he had to be Dutch! We eventually got round to telling him about the effect the recent documentary had on us and how my wife thought we should enrol. He advised us to write to the head office in Cologne. We did not get in touch again. It was him who actually chased us up. Also one evening we visited a friend in Wuppertal who had once been in The Salvation Army and he too encouraged us to take on the uniform and all the

Join the Salvation Army! Not a Chance!

principles that it represented under its slogan 'Soup, Soap and Salvation'.

When we got home that evening there in the letterbox was a copy of *The War Cry*, the Salvation Army newspaper, and written on it in Dutch was a message from Eddie Pauwel asking what stage we had reached enrolling and when were we coming to obey God's command. That clinched it for me. I was ready to take up his sword and become one of God's soldiers.

I was ready and willing but one thing still stood in my way from becoming part of the Salvation Army. I was addicted to smoking and smoking was against the strict principles of the movement.

Every member of The Salvation Army was duty-bound to live a life of propriety free from the influence of alcohol and nicotine and therefore worthy of Jesus Christ. As true upstanding examples of clean living they would draw attention to the movement and encourage others to emulate this way of life. I had a problem when it came to renouncing nicotine. I tried every means of stopping. Neither willpower nor prayer worked. I asked Doris to pray for me, and then the parish including the minister, but it brought no relief. A youth worker dared to tell me that I could go through the motions of trying to stop smoking but it would not work because the truth of the matter was that I did not want to stop and I would therefore never succeed. I almost took a swipe at him for having the audacity to say this to me but on reflection I knew he had a point. I

Hallelujah Joe

worked out that every morning first thing I took a quarter of an hour cigarette break and I was therefore diddling my employers out of fifteen minutes wages. I thought more people ought to look at it in this light and maybe even smoking should be banned at work. But what was I going to do about stopping? I decided if I could not break the habit mentally then I would try physical means. I therefore went to the chemists and bought six sticks of anti-smoking chewing gum for the equivalent of over an hour's wage, which was supposedly guaranteed to help you stop the same day. I chewed the lot for over an hour before spitting it out but when I then tried a cigarette it tasted better than ever. Once again I had been taken in and deceived by the outside world.

That night I sat down and made pact with God. I told him that if he wanted me to join The Salvation Army he had to help by taking away my craving for cigarettes. If he did not do this for me I would not go. And then I helped God intervene by throwing my tobacco and roll-ups into the bin, and carrying the rubbish out to the outside bin and dumping it. My wife could hardly believe I had actually taken the rubbish out far less chucked my cigarettes away and she had little faith in it working. However, the next morning a colleague asked me whether I was sick because he had noticed that I had not been smoking. I told him that as of eight o'clock the previous night I had given up. He almost split his sides laughing but I had the last laugh. God kept his part of the pact.

Chapter Twenty-three

HALLELUJAH

Like most people we knew relatively little about The Salvation Army. I had met a few women officers on their collection rounds or seen them on street corners singing their Bible songs. I knew that they had gone into areas like St Pauli and helped prostitutes. But that was not very much knowledge on which to found a future so we went about gathering more information.

We discovered The Salvation Army is an evangelical free church active in social welfare work which was founded in England in the middle of the 19th century by a Methodist minister from Nottingham, William Booth (1829–1912). He was mightily concerned about the extent of human suffering in the world, especially the poverty amongst the working classes in Victorian England, but he also cared passionately about their lack of spiritual and moral fibre due to a lack of instruction. He felt they were God's lost sheep and it was his responsibility to bring them back into the fold. Along with his wife Catherine he took it upon himself to pass on the message of Christ to the poor and to help the neediest. In a tent in the East End, one of the poorest districts in the city of London, and later in

Hallelujah Joe

a converted pub, he preached evangelism to ever increasing audiences. At the same time he built up the soup kitchen and grocery shops where the poor could buy provisions at honest prices.

Very early on in life Booth recognized the evil of alcohol. He saw how men often spent their whole meagre wage on beer or spirits leaving their womenfolk and children homeless with no other alternative but to find shelter under bridges. It was during a life of compassionate evangelism that Booth coined memorable sayings such as: 'You cannot preach to a hungry man or one with cold feet'; and 'Go for souls, and go for the worst.' The Army was known also for its saying: 'Soup, Soap and Salvation.'

With the greatest possible fervour William Booth called out for a return to God, for converts to step forward and enter his Kingdom. He tried to send these new Christians to the churches, but they found little welcome and William Booth needed their help in the growing Christian Mission as the Army was first called. What he needed to help him in his cause was a mobile, Christian front line formed of readily recognizable followers who could quickly intervene at any given time whenever the need arose. This is how The Salvation Army came into being in 1865 with Booth as its first General, although the movement's title – and his – was first used in 1878.

The military title given to the movement was meant to draw a parallel to the war against evil which was the Salvationists' mission. This is still the

Hallelujah

aim nowadays and the military correlations are still maintained. The Army's newspaper is entitled *The War Cry*, area branches are called corps, members of the corps are soldiers, the official ministers are officers, the ecclesiastical office is the Headquarters and the voluntary contributors are patrons. If you want to join its ranks you enrol and when you die you are 'promoted to Glory'. The movement quickly spread through England and later travelled abroad. William and Catherine Booth brushed away centuries of church traditions in order to save people from evil. 'My best men are women', he once said and introduced sex equality to his officer-ranks. Catherine Booth was one of the first women to preach, at that time a giant leap forward for the female race. Soon The Salvation Army used brass bands to link popular folk music to the Christian message in the eyes of the people. Booth could not see why the Devil should have all the good music. The temperance movement grew so strong that the breweries and pubs feared closure and an opposition movement of hardy drinkers formed and called themselves the Skeleton Army. Taking to the streets with flags and cudgels as well as musical instruments they engaged in battles against God's soldiers and in those days brutally assaulted the salvationsts.

These days of open aggression are thankfully over. The Salvation Army has long since completed its triumphal march around the world. It is basically a church for humble people who enter into Christianity with their sleeves rolled up, according

Hallelujah Joe

to Eva Burrows, the General in charge of over three million troops in ninety countries worldwide. Members of The Salvation Army are still out in the front line wherever sin subjugates humanity, whether it is amongst the poor in third world countries, amongst the homeless in cities, amongst the ill and infirm, in prisons, homes or in the streets. And members of The Salvation Army always draw attention to themselves through their cheerful disposition and evident joy of life through Christ. Their services in which they unmistakably invite people to join them in Christ, are happy celebrations with lively music and loud enthusiastic shouts of Hallelujah. These were the people that we Scharwähters were to join.

Chapter Twenty-four

ENROLLED

The National Headquarters in Cologne took some time to reply to our letter offering our services. I had enclosed a few newspaper clippings vouching for my good work to date. They sent a stalling letter thanking us for our kind interest but urging us to be patient because their General Secretary, Lieutenant-Colonel John Dale, was still on holiday. Four weeks passed before we received an invitation to meet him in Cologne.

He was an Englishman who had come to Germany as a Salvation Army Officer at the end of the Second World War just as the allied troops were retreating and later he was awarded the highest state decoration for decades of unfailing dedicated service. This man with an unmistakable English accent radiated a zest for life and true Christian optimism. He knew all about The Salvation Army better than anyone else and he also understood the toil it imposed upon its own ranks. But he was nevertheless genuinely thrilled that my wife and I wanted to enrol in the service of Christ. He advised us to seek out a suitable corps and set to work.

That was easier said than done. The first corps we tried hardly acknowledged our presence. They spoke to us politely but when my wife tried to continue the conversation she found that their attention had already shifted elsewhere.

Finally we found a tiny corps in Wuppertal-Elberfeld. The leader was out on the streets all on her own and as soon as we spoke to her we knew at once we were in the right place. We started by helping out in the church services, open air meetings and in the economic drives such as selling *The War Cry* in the local pubs. The next step was being made recruits and having passed muster we were then enrolled as soldiers into The Salvation Army. We then bought our uniforms and truly belonged to the corps.

Nevertheless, around this time I was gradually becoming more and more disillusioned with Christianity, and my faith was in a crisis. I had been trying desperately to convince people to believe in God but no matter how much energy I expended I had not been successful. This detracted from my own joy at being a Christian and I began to think it was all too much of a palaver.

The crisis was eased, however, by talking at length to a preacher I met on one of my prison journeys. He advised me to talk less abstractly about the Christian message of love, freedom and forgiveness, but more rooted to my own personal experience of God and how he changed my life for the better. We prayed together for the power of God to take its effect through me to carry on his work here on earth. The preacher said he would bless me by laying his

Enrolled

hands on me as outlined in the Bible and that I would be filled with an inner joy, and in so doing it was just as he had said.

Later I met a school friend who was astounded to catch sight of me in a Salvation Army uniform. I suggested that we went somewhere to talk about it. I told him everything and afterwards we prayed together and he became a Christian there and then. This was a completely new experience for me. I went home and told my wife what had happened and asked her to forgive me for all the things I had done wrong up until that point. I was then possessed with an inner happiness that until this day has never left me.

Our promotion within The Salvation Army moved quite quickly. Soon we were candidates for officer training in Bochum to learn how to preach sermons. Married couples who want to attain this higher Salvation Army grading within the ministry had both to undertake the religious teaching and become ordained because later in service men and women had exactly the same duties to fulfil. This is what we were aiming to achieve and started mental preparations towards.

Chapter Twenty-five
THE SAGA OF MY DRIVING LICENCE

There was still one thing that nagged at my conscience. Since my youth my greatest passion in life had been driving. I sat behind a steering wheel for the first time when I was only sixteen years old and of course I did not then have a driving licence but I took to the roads without any problem. Although I drove a lot I never actually got round to sitting my driving test. Even after becoming a Christian and my final release from prison I continued to drive without a licence.

When I was working in the steelworks I caused an accident one day. I panicked and failed to stop because I was scared that it would finally be discovered that I did not hold a licence and my parole would be endangered. Back safely at home I wrestled with my bad conscience until finally I had to confess to my wife what I had done. Until then she had no idea that I had not passed my test. I went to the police and gave myself up. A new charge was brought against me for illegal driving and a hit-and-run accident. But my probation officer was a great source of support and thought that I had made so

The Saga of My Driving Licence

much progress in my life that I would probably be awarded probation a second time. The trial took place and the judge announced that it would be a very unusual occurrence for a person with my long list of previous offenses not be re-sentenced but because my life was now following such an orderly path he would grant me a further probationary period. It was as if a ton weight had lifted from me. The sentence of eight months' imprisonment was suspended to five years' probation.

From then on I no longer took the wheel until one disastrous day when fate stepped in. We were at the time members of The Salvation Army awaiting openings on the next officer training course. My wife was driving myself and our two-year-old son, Carsten, down to Switzerland on holiday when we hit some terrible bad weather. It was bucketing down and the whole road was waterlogged. My wife was heading towards a rest area to stop but the brakes failed when she tried to slow down. We were thrown into shock. The little one started to cry and in a panic I shouted to my wife to steer to the side. In so doing we came to a halt. My wife had managed to avert a tragedy.

First of all she had to attend to Carsten for he was hysterical and needed his nappy changed. Meanwhile I had to check out the brakes so I asked for the car keys and hopped it into reverse and drove backwards out of the picnic area and forwards again just to test if they were still working. A brown Mercedes pulled up beside me and on exchanging a few pleasantries

Hallelujah Joe

asked for my papers. I had not realized at first that they were plain clothes policemen. I told them it was my wife they needed to see and she would just be a moment. They told me that the rear left light was not working and I thought now we were in for it.

Then the whole hullabaloo broke loose. My wife started to cry thinking that I had been detected. I had reconciled myself to the worst and tried my best to console her telling her that we would put our trust in God that everything would work out for the best. We clung to this hope but we did not tell anyone about it, not even The Salvation Army.

We were already in charge of a little community when we received the summons. I wrote a letter to the examining magistrate explaining the mitigating circumstances. Without any great expectations I requested that the charge be dropped but this could not be done and the case continued.

The day of the court hearing finally came and my wife, Carsten and myself drove there together. Carsten played on the floor of the court room whilst the proceedings went on. My defence lawyer looked at me sharply on arrival and asked why I had not worn my Salvation Army uniform. I was quick to retort that it was me and not The Salvation Army that was on trial that day. I had very negative vibes about the whole episode thinking that I would probably go straight back to jail. I had even thought about doing a bunk.

I was asked to recount the sequence of events leading up to the offence. I told him about the

The Saga of My Driving Licence

dreadful weather conditions, how the road lay under water, how it was an emergency because our brakes had failed and how I had only taken the wheel to test them out. I was not allowed to finish my speech but asked to step down from the bench for the next witness to be called. The police verified my account of the state of the weather saying that night they were very busy because of the road conditions. When asked whether they had seen me come out and in of the parking place they admitted to only seeing a car with a faulty rear light and not the driver and they had as a matter of routine asked to see our papers. The judge then interrupted the hearing and sent us out of the courtroom. I was convinced that this was the end. Nothing could happen to save me now. Ten minutes later we were admitted back into the courtroom and the judge started to pronounce the verdict. I was shocked because the prosecuting attorney had not yet said his piece and even more astounded to hear the pronouncement of 'Case dismissed'.

I was mightily relieved for this judgment was the only chance I had of maintaining my parole. The judge went on to say that he would have behaved in exactly the same manner if put in a similar situation. It was an emergency and safety was the first consideration. He just wanted to see how I would react under the burden of prosecution. He commended me for facing up to the situation bravely and believed that I had chosen the right path through The Salvation Army to overcome my past.

Chapter Twenty-six

SERVING THE LORD
AND MORE

Doris and I were now candidates for the officer training school. But we did not sit back and relax with our hands in our laps. We wanted to prove ourselves and experience as much as we could on the practical side. We knew we would be treated to enough theory at the training school in Bochum whether it be furthering our knowledge of the Bible, theology, church history or homiletics (the art of teaching or writing sermons).

We were pleased to be working at the side of our discoverer, Eddie Pauwels, in his corps in Dortmund. He was a man of action and he had great faith in the power of God and was full of optimism. On the very first day he rented a single room in a house for the homeless he would already be looking forward three months hence to when he would fill the whole house with needy people off the streets. And often he made his dreams reality. I learnt everything about what it is to serve in The Salvation Army from him, learning from the bottom up. I worked in his model home for social dropouts. In the evenings we scoured every inch of the area

Serving the Lord and More

around the station in search of people lying in corners just to prove to them that we cared enough to look for them and find them and offered help where necessary. On Sundays we provided them with our now famous soup or sausage and salad. Not exactly *nouvelle cuisine* but the people who came were full of gratitude and love. This practical means of extending brotherly love to others had a positive effect on a number of people. They understood and experienced for themselves that Jesus can save lives even today. Not just through our actions but also through his sermons. I will never forget the methods of one old Salvation Army evangelist who would simply sit down before people, stretch out his hand and invite them to come to Jesus.

Of course, there were a lot of things that I found irritating. For instance, I was shocked that The Salvation Army was prepared to put us in charge of a corps after only six months. We were first asked to join in the ongoing work at a social rehabilitation centre for former people of no fixed abode and alcoholics, and then we were actually asked to lead a community in Düsseldorf.

The training was tough but very educational. I remember one evening after going round all the pubs selling our newspaper and offering spiritual guidance to those in need I travelled through an area of great deprivation on my moped, where lots of homeless slept out. Some of them were lying there in the cold and wet with only a blanket for protection. One of them addressed me asking what I knew of life,

Hallelujah Joe

looking so spick-and-span in my uniform. I told him my life history. We kept in touch for a long time afterwards and it was rewarding to watch how changed this man became. Today he lives a respectable, middle-class life.

You can all too easily become too bourgeois, even in The Salvation Army believe it or not. In one corps the local establishment were against allowing the homeless to take part – any part – in their dignified meetings and thought that they needed to set up separate church services for them. The same applied to the open-air meetings, which are in fact an ideal means of attracting people who never otherwise go to church – the overriding majority – and letting them hear about the Christian message. What is most important is how the message is put across. I personally could never see the benefit of some of the old ways of working within The Salvation Army such as elderly members standing rigid at a street corner singing obscure songs to an out of tune guitar and thus making fools of themselves. I agree The Salvation Army belongs out on the streets, for that is where it originated, but at the same time some thought ought to be injected into the movement as to how to make people contemplate a life with Jesus instead of just making them screw up their noses at the sight of us. I built up a good relationship with Christian youth groups who spread the word of God through street pantomimes or dances. There are so many people in this world who cannot see any point to their lives and who are seeking God but do not

Serving the Lord and More

know where to find him. That is why The Salvation Army should be visible and ready to be of assistance.

Inge Brück, a renowned singer who had not only given concerts for The Salvation Army in Düsseldorf but had also walked the streets with us to help us in our mission, pointed us in the direction of an actor who was a chronic alcoholic. When we visited him we found him in a state of delirium, so we took him home and put him up in our children's room. Still trembling from withdrawal symptoms he accompanied us to church later that evening. I could not offer him any more constructive advice as to how to overcome his drinking problem and recommended that he see a psychiatrist. But I was furious when I heard that this psychiatrist had simply told him to go to a whorehouse and sleep with a woman and then he would be a normal person again. I told him I had a better solution to accept Christ and begin a new life through him just as I had done.

Soon the time came to take up our officer training. Our class year was given the attractive name 'Soldiers of God', and at thirty-five I was once more sitting down at a school bench, the only male amongst nine women. It was not easy to readjust. Much of the theory passed over my head as I was more in favour of practical methods. I was helped a great deal and given moral support by our teacher, Major Mathilde Schmidt. She was a slight, inconspicuous but very clever woman from North Germany who to the outside world appeared shy. We could not be more different as people. She somehow managed not to

Hallelujah Joe

quarrel or go against me once in the whole training period. For that alone she won my wholehearted respect. I not only held her in the highest esteem but she forged a place in my heart.

She was very interested in my past and went with me to Frankfurt to seek out my old stomping ground, the station area. We were sitting in a pub when a couple of fellows came in who recognized me from my pimping days. They tried immediately to poke fun at me, laughing at the fact that Dutch Joe as now in the Sally Army and inferring that I was some holy man. The pub owner's wife was quick to intervene. She dashed from behind the bar and slapped the one who had insulted me across the face and banned them both from her pub, saying that when they had managed to make a go of life like me then only then were they welcome to come back.

After two years of officer training the big day of our ordination was fast approaching on 6 June 1981. It was not the celebrations with the magnificent trooping of the cadets and future officers that moved me but the day we took our vows, a day of tranquillity four days beforehand. It was marked by silent worship, Bible contemplation, prayer intervals and hours of silence offering plenty of time in which to think over carefully and in all seriousness whether The Salvation Army really was the right place for me. It was more than a conscious decision on a career path, which is an important factor in everyone's life, it was a matter of affirming my calling. At the end of the day we had to take our

Serving the Lord and More

vows by signing a covenant to serve God faithfully and constantly within The Salvation Army.

I took a long time to think it over, as did my wife. I looked back over my life until that point through childhood, youth and adulthood through all life's disappointments, rejections and confusion, the homes, prisons, whorehouses and criminal bars. But amidst all this shone a new beginning. The joy and thankfulness at my new life with Doris and the children, and above all with Jesus. My life that once was lost was born again. I along with others had squandered this precious gift of life in the past but now God had made me whole again. I could see no reason not to dedicate the rest of my life to his service and help others in his name.

For over a quarter of an hour I knelt at the prayer bench of The Salvation Army. Then when I had found my inner peace I stood up to sign my covenant. God had the final stroke. He wiped out the name Dutch Joe and gave me another: 'Hallelujah Joe'.

Hallelujah Joe

EPILOGUE

This is my life history. A story of a criminal who became a Christian. But this is by no means the end. My life is only just beginning, veering away from its bent course on to the straight and narrow, and it is no less exciting as a consequence.

I am now setting out to say to other people that they too can alter their lives. There are no hopeless cases. Every person is valued by God and is too precious to be allowed to perish or fall by the wayside.

I continue to travel throughout the country speaking to all sorts of people – tramps, prostitutes, jailbirds, pimps, bikers. These people who live on the edge or outside society and those who have chosen to opt out. On the other hand I also speak to people with their feet firmly placed in respected society, managers, directors, decent, ordinary citizens. These people who are successful, well-off and well-fed. I am speaking about people who never set foot inside church and also Christians who have become self-satisfied and too comfortable with their lot. It is clear to me that both social groupings lack knowledge of true life. Behind their masks it is easy to detect doubt, resignation, and bitterness.

I know that they are searching for the truth and for eternal life. Only one person can give this to them: Jesus Christ.